Contents

KT-116-331

Sculptor of our times

" *'Time will show that Moore and Picasso have been the two greatest figures in modern art.'* "

John Read, art historian and friend of Henry Moore, 1979

Henry Moore stands like one of his own colossal works as the world's foremost modern sculptor. While many artists' greatest efforts are confined to museums and art galleries, or buried away in private collections, much of Moore's work is 'public' – decorating parks, squares, churches, streets and buildings.

Henry Moore pictured in his London studio in 1927–28, surrounded by finished pieces and several 'works in progress'.

In the public eye

When we talk about 'public sculpture' we often have an idea fixed in our minds. We think of statues of once-famous generals and civic dignitaries standing forlornly in parks and squares, their deeds forgotten and their presence appreciated only by the pigeons that perch on them. Almost single-handedly, Henry Moore rescued sculpture as the work of artists. He made it one of the most **radical** and in many ways controversial art forms, and put art directly into the public domain. And, whether they loved it or hated it, the public formed strong opinions about his work. As Moore himself said, 'Who is wrong? Is it me or them?'

CREATIVE LIVES

Henry Moore

JEREMY WALLIS

Heinemann
LIBRARY

H **www.heinemann.co.uk/library**
Visit our website to find out more information about **Heinemann Library** books.

To order:
☎ Phone 44 (0) 1865 888066
▤ Send a fax to 44 (0) 1865 314091
💻 Visit the Heinemann Bookshop at www.heinemann.co.uk/library to browse our catalogue and order online.

First published in Great Britain by Heinemann Library, Halley Court, Jordan Hill, Oxford OX2 8EJ, part of Harcourt Education. Heinemann is a registered trademark of Harcourt Education Ltd.

OXFORD MELBOURNE AUCKLAND JOHANNESBURG BLANTYRE GABORONE IBADAN PORTSMOUTH NH (USA) CHICAGO

Designed by Tinstar Design (www.tinstar.co.uk)
Originated by Ambassador Litho Ltd.
Printed and bound in Hong Kong/China

ISBN 0 431 13984 9 (hardback)   ISBN 0 431 13991 1 (paperback)
06 05 04 03 02   06 05 04 03
10 9 8 7 6 5 4 3 2 1   10 9 8 7 6 5 4 3 2 1

British Library Cataloguing in Publication Data
Wallis, Jeremy
     Henry Moore. – (Creative lives)
     1.Moore, Henry, 1898-1986 – Juvenile literature
     2.Sculptors – England – Biography – Juvenile literature
     I.Title
     730.9'2

Acknowledgements
The Publishers would like to thank the following for permission to reproduce photographs: Archivio Fotografico Ca Pesaro: p39; Henry Moore Foundation; pp9, 38; Hulton Getty: pp13, 17; John Hedgecoe: p54; Leeds University/ Eric Gill: p16; Leeds Museums & Galleries (Henry Moore Institute): p50; The Art Archive: pp22, 34; The Henry Moore Foundation: pp4, 6, 7, 8, 11, 12, 14, 19, 20, 25, 27, 28, 29, 30, 33, 35, 37, 40, 41, 43, 44, 47, 48, 52, Michel Muller pp5, 24, 51. Cover photograph reproduced with permission of John Hedgecoe.

Our thanks to John Hedgecoe and Chrysalis Books/Collins & Brown for permission to use extracts from Henry Moore: *My Ideas, Inspiration and Life as an Artist*.

Our thanks to Angela Dyer for her comments in the preparation of this book.

Any words appearing in the text in bold, **like this**, are explained in the Glossary.

Though best known for his sculpture, Moore was also an accomplished painter, etcher and drawer. It was the drawings he made as an **official war artist** during World War II that first brought him public acclaim.

Image and inspiration

As with many artists, it is important to distinguish between myth and truth when studying the life of Henry Moore. He challenges our ideas about typical artists: as eccentrics living 'on the edge', tormented by their imagination. Though world-famous in his lifetime, Henry Moore was solid, calm and unassuming, and never given to self-important theorizing. Although he was a radical figure in Britain's vibrant art scene in the years following World War I, he liked to project the image of a **working-class** Yorkshireman: a plain-speaking chap who, through hard work and good fortune, had achieved his life's ambition and could support his family by doing what he loved best. Moore's clothes were always conservative: jacket, flannel trousers, shirt and tie. He never wore eccentric dress and even in the 1930s, when there was a fashion for all things French among his circle, he didn't take to wearing a beret!

Moore's artistic inspirations were very wide-ranging. They included nature and natural forms, Greek myths and ancient Greek art, the native art of Latin America and Africa, modern art movements, war, his own childhood and youth, and his experience of family life and parenthood.

Family Group, 1948–49. After the birth of his daughter, Mary, the family became one of Henry Moore's favourite subjects.

Childhood

Henry Moore was born on 30 July 1898, in Castleford, West Yorkshire, the seventh of eight children. The entire Moore family – two adults and eight children – shared a redbrick terrace, 'back-to-back' house, typical of the area. It had two rooms up and two rooms down, plus a cellar. The front parlour was the 'respectable' room, kept clean for Sundays and for visitors. The back room was for everything else – sitting, cooking, eating and bathing. A small space shared by so many demanded patience and tolerance.

Henry's parents

Often described in biographies of Henry Moore as 'a miner', Henry's father, Raymond Spencer Moore, worked in the pit but improved himself by mastering, without educational support, the mathematical and technical knowledge he needed to become a mining engineer. He read widely and knew all of Shakespeare's works, and taught himself to play the violin.

Henry Moore as a boy. By the age of eleven, Henry had decided he wanted to be a sculptor.

Henry reflected on the character of his father during a miners' strike in 1906, when Henry was eight: 'He did odd jobs, mended shoes, any jobs at all. He was good with his hands. He was politically active and used to hold meetings in our front room… We had a very thin time, but my father was unbelievably resilient and ambitious for his children. He had had to learn everything himself, from books and so on… But he had tremendous hopes for his children.'

Henry's parents, Raymond and Mary Moore. Henry always spoke of his parents with nothing but the highest regard.

Raymond Moore believed that education was the best chance **working-class** children had of improving their prospects and escaping a future working down the **pit**. He encouraged all his children to study and sit the **scholarship** exam for the local **grammar school**. Two of Henry's sisters and a brother went on to college and became teachers.

Of his mother, Mary, Moore said, 'She had tremendous physical stamina. She used to work from morning to night until she was well over 70.'

> " Moore wrote of his childhood: *'I had a happy childhood, full of physical enjoyment and exercise. I enjoyed all the... fights as well. I fought one boy with my hand tied behind me – I said I could beat you one-handed. You had to stand up for yourself, it was daft if you didn't.'* "

Life in Castleford

By all accounts Henry's childhood was happy and free of complications. Only the death of his younger sister, Elsie, cast a shadow over a youth spent exploring canals, **slagheaps** and woodland, and playing children's games in the streets of Castleford. It was a much more simple time than today, before parental fear and the motor car drove children from the streets, alleys and common land.

It was also a life lived closer to the raw edges of the man-made environment. Moore wrote: 'As children we'd go to the **slaughterhouse**... You could stand and see them fell the cow, the sheep, or the bull with an axe with a point at one end and blade on the other... It was a gruesome sight but we'd say, "Let's go and watch the kill".'

Now more a suburb of the city of Leeds, Castleford was then a settlement in its own right. Coal was the backbone of the town's economy and though the pits are now gone the land still bears their mark – huge spoil-tips, or slagheaps. These stand like relics of an ancient civilization, softening under a carpet of grass and trees. They are one of the first and strongest memories of Castleford that Moore recalled: 'Like pyramids, like mountains, artificial mountains... We played about them, and got very dirty.'

Adel Woods, near Leeds, is an area with several extraordinary rock formations. Henry visited Adel Woods a number of times with both the school and his father. Years later Henry claimed these bizarre formations had influenced his work.

Play was a time of exploration and experimentation. Moore later acknowledged it had been essential to his development as an artist: in his understanding of nature and the development of his imagination. Childhood games also provoked his interest in modelling with clay. In a nearby quarry, Henry and his friends would play about with the clay and make what they called 'touchstone ovens' – little decorated boxes with chimneys and a hole in the side. They would light small fires in them and warm their hands in the winter.

Nature was significant to the young Moore. Close to Castleford were miles of countryside that were a welcome retreat from the dirt and grime of the town's back streets. It was here that Henry began to

Stone effigies from Methley Church, Castleford. These were the first real sculptures that Henry had seen. He later recalled: 'I was very impressed by the recumbent figures, particularly of the woman's head.'

> " *'It was a great excitement for me to discover... form as a three-dimensional reality... and the way light revealed form.'*
> Henry Moore, 1985 "

appreciate the beauty of the natural environment. 'I think I was always aware of the trees and branches, and the way they responded to environmental forces...,' he recalled. He and his friends would walk miles into the countryside, to explore the woodland and play on the banks and towpaths of the Calder Canal. He came to realize that natural shapes had three dimensions and that the light at different times of the day or season changed them.

Schooldays

As a boy, Henry was enrolled at the local primary school and also attended **Sunday school** at a nearby chapel. By the age of ten, Moore found he took great pleasure from art – from drawing classes and from carving old bits of wood and stone. At Sunday school his teacher told a story of the Italian artist Michelangelo taking guidance on a piece he was sculpting from a passing stranger. 'So there you are,' she said. 'The greatest sculptor in the world taking advice from a stranger.' For Henry the story was irrelevant – what stuck in his mind was the phrase 'the greatest sculptor in the world'. From that moment Henry knew what he wanted to be: a sculptor.

Henry's chances of fulfilling his dream were not as gloomy as they might first appear. While there were few places in Britain to study sculpture at that time – and all of them in London – there were plenty of examples of sculpture all around him.

Henry failed his grammar school examinations but his father made him sit them again. He passed and was admitted to Castleford Secondary School, where he met two people who were to have a profound influence upon him: Mr T.R. Dawes, the headteacher, and Miss Alice Gostick, the art teacher.

Mr Dawes was a strong believer in education of the broadest and truest kind. He regularly organized school outings to old churches and abbey ruins – 'more sculpture than architecture,' Moore recalled.

Alice Gostick quickly recognized Moore's talent. In turn she became the boy's heroine and stimulated his interest in art. She had travelled a lot and told her pupils of the sculpture and paintings she had seen in Florence and London. She would invite them to her house for tea and lend them books. Alice Gostick introduced Henry to works of art he had not seen or heard of before. 'She was one of the biggest influences on the direction I took,' he later wrote.

Henry's first serious woodcarving was the school memorial for former pupils wounded or killed in the early years of World War I. Miss Gostick lent him the tools; he had only used a penknife before. She remained a close friend and their correspondence lasted until her death 50 years later.

The Castleford Secondary School Roll of Honour pays tribute to former pupils of the school killed or wounded in the first years of World War I. It was Henry's first real piece of carving.

Alice Gostick's art and pottery class. Even after leaving secondary school, Henry continued to attend Miss Gostick's classes as a student. Moore sits in the front row, on the left.

Henry's desire to become a sculptor was greeted coolly by his family, however. He wanted to go to art college, but his father persuaded him that it would be better if he qualified as a teacher like several of his brothers and sisters, and so have something to fall back on. Henry himself recognized that life as an artist would be a struggle and that teaching would be a means of earning a living – indeed, he passed on his father's advice to his own students in later years.

From 1914, World War I took many adult teachers from the classroom and put them in military service. To fill the gap, **student teachers** were recruited and trained. In 1915 Henry began working as a student teacher at the same primary school he had attended. He was seventeen years old. There was, it seemed, nothing that would disturb the ordered tranquillity of his Castleford life.

War and peace

Competition between the European **empires** had grown for years. In 1914 the steps towards war quickened. In June of that year, Serbian **nationalists** assassinated the Austrian heir to the throne. Austria-Hungary then declared war on Serbia and in support of Austria-Hungary, Germany declared war on Russia and France. Germany hoped Britain would remain neutral but attacked France through Belgium, an ally of Britain. Britain declared war.

Initially there had been a lot of enthusiasm for war and a naive belief that the conflict 'would all be over by Christmas'. However, as war dragged on, people resigned themselves to the **trench**-bound slaughter. In the Battle of the Somme, between July and November 1916, wave after wave of troops commanded by the British Commander-in-Chief, Douglas Haig, marched straight into German machine-gun fire. When the attack was finally abandoned, an advance of less than 16 kilometres had cost the British and German armies over a million casualties. It had become the bloodiest battle in world history. By the end of the war in 1918, over 10 million combatants worldwide had been killed and 20 million injured.

A British trench in World War I. Conditions in the trenches were terrible, soldiers often being up to their knees in mud and water. Infestations of lice and rats were commonplace.

Joining the army

Though still a **student teacher**, Moore intended to take a place at the Leeds College of Art. But the setbacks of 1916 put everything at risk. Volunteers had formed the backbone of the British army until the terrible slaughter of the summer. In autumn the British government introduced **conscription** for all men aged eighteen and a half or over.

Moore's father realized that if Henry beat the inevitable summons to serve by volunteering, then he would have a say in his choice of regiment. At the age of eighteen he was packed off to London. He did not mind too much; teaching was, he thought, too hard a career.

At that time many regiments and battalions were organized by professions or districts – the so-called 'pals' battalions'. Moore tried to get into the Artists' Rifles, but was turned down for being too short. He joined the Civil Service Rifles (15th London Regiment), which was understrength, instead. As the youngest of his regiment, Moore thought the army was 'just like a bigger family'. He also used his time in London to visit the British Museum and the National Gallery.

Henry Moore and his company in uniform. Moore sits bottom right in the photograph.

Moore became a machine-gunner and was sent to France in 1917 to join the 1st Battalion of the Civil Service Rifles. He spent a lot of time drawing – flowers, trees, huts, ruins, people picking lice off their clothes – before being sent into action at Cambrai.

Planned as a major push using the recently invented tanks, the Battle of Cambrai seemed to start well. But as the Civil Service Rifles joined the battle, things went badly wrong. A German counterattack, supported by cannons, aircraft and gas, cut Moore's regiment off.

Moore, despite the horror and perhaps because of his youth, nurtured dreams of winning a medal. He wanted to shoot down enemy aircraft. To avoid bringing enemy fire down upon his comrades, he volunteered to take his heavy machine gun to a nearby shell-hole. But his brave ambitions came to nothing – the aircraft zipped over too fast to be hit and the soldier carrying Moore's ammunition carrier got so drunk on rum that Moore had to sit on the bottle to stop him drinking it all.

In the push to close the gap opened by the Germans, Moore was then caught in several mustard-gas attacks. Despite gas masks, the toxic effects of the gas built up in his system until he became very ill. Coughing and spluttering, he was sent with other casualties, many of them blinded by the gas, to a field hospital. The soldiers' uniforms had become so saturated with gas that several medical orderlies were themselves overcome.

His lungs seriously injured, Moore was forced to spend two months in hospital. He later recalled that of the 400 who went out, only 42 came back. But despite his experiences Moore was not traumatized. Instead he displayed a cool and almost fatalistic steadiness of character.

After leaving hospital, Moore was made an Army PTI (Physical Training Instructor). Discharged from the army in February 1919, he returned home and within a month was teaching at his old school. He was now 20 years old.

Eric Gill's controversial war memorial at Leeds University (see page 58). Showing the biblical story of Jesus driving the money changers from the temple, it demonstrated Gill's contempt for those who had profited and grown rich from the war.

Leeds College of Art

After the war the government gave out ex-servicemen's grants – financial help to people whose education had been disrupted. Moore applied for one and it enabled him to go to Leeds College of Art. By now he was mature and experienced enough to know and demand what he wanted, and he wanted to be a sculptor. There were no sculpture courses at the college, so a new teacher, who had just left the Royal College of Art in London, was brought in specially – and Moore was his only student.

While attending college, Moore lived at home in Castleford, running for the train to Leeds every morning. He was a very conscientious student, determined to achieve the high marks he needed to get a **scholarship** to the Royal College of Art. In the evenings he returned to Castleford, to attend Alice Gostick's pottery classes.

Sir Michael Sadler, the vice-chancellor (assistant head) of Leeds University and the art critic Roger Fry (see box opposite) were a major influence on Moore. He was especially excited when he read Fry's *Vision and Design*, a collection of essays published in 1920. Two particularly influential essays were on African sculpture and ancient American art. These stimulated Moore's interest in **primitive art**, at that time not featured on the college curriculum.

At Leeds Moore met Barbara Hepworth (see page 58). 'I became a bit sweet on her and we went out together,' he confessed. Hepworth, herself the child of a **working-class** family, was following a foundation course in art and aspired to become a sculptor. They both won scholarships from Leeds to the Royal College of Art in London, and lived near each other among a group of artists and intellectuals in Hampstead in the early 1930s.

Born in Wakefield, West Yorkshire, Barbara Hepworth also became a sculptor. She and Moore developed a long artistic association and friendship.

Art and sculpture in Leeds

Sir Michael Sadler, the vice-chancellor of Leeds University (of which Leeds College of Art was part) between 1911 and 1923, was a keen collector of modern art. He bought works by painters such as Cézanne, Gauguin and Van Gogh. He also had many examples of African carving, well before it had gained acceptance in Britain. Most British people, even those in London, were suspicious of art, especially sculpture, because it was seen as overtly sexual and was out of step with the prudishness of the times. The people of Leeds, however, developed a 'genuine enthusiastic intellectual and spiritual life', and were very interested in art, according to the influential art critic Roger Fry.

Royal College of Art

In 1921 Moore earned a Royal Exhibition scholarship to study at the prestigious Royal College of Art (RCA) in London. He rented a small room in Sydney Street, Chelsea. Although it was tiny, it was the first room Moore had ever had to himself and he loved it. The only dark cloud was the death of his father in 1922, soon after he had enrolled at the RCA.

For many years ancient Greek art was held up as the only standard of excellence. Like other young artists, Moore rejected this and looked for other sources of inspiration. He was inspired by Roger Fry's book (see page 16), and studied the huge collection of primitive art at the British Museum at first hand. Moore grew to believe that the ancient Greek ideal in art, of realistic representation, was 'only a digression from the main world tradition of sculpture'. He also grasped the fact that the medieval pieces he had seen, such as those in Methley Church (see page 9), were part of this main world tradition.

Although Moore shared his contemporaries' enthusiasm for African art, he found himself drawn to Latin American sculpture. He was quietly pleased to follow a less well-trodden path. In his imagination and outlook Moore was already ahead of most of his teachers, but he realized that he had a lot to learn, both as an artist and as a craftsman. For his first two years at the RCA he was taught life-drawing by another sculptor, Leon Underwood, himself passionate about the importance of drawing. In sculpture classes Moore was taught by Francis Derwent Wood, who appreciated the young Yorkshireman's enthusiasm and skill, if not his designs.

Moore recognized that he had to learn the technical skills of the sculptor as they were taught at the RCA, and spent years emulating the work of the **classical** European artists. Whenever he got the chance, however, he completed pieces and drawings inspired by the primitive works he saw in the British Museum: art which was derided by one of his professors as 'garbage'.

At this time, the principal of the RCA was Sir William Rothenstein. He believed in looking outward to the whole world of art – he had known the great artists Edgar Degas and Auguste Rodin (see page 58), and was acquainted with many other leading figures of art, literature and culture. Rothenstein proved to be an invaluable ally. Moore later wrote, 'Rothenstein was from a rich, Jewish wool family from Yorkshire... Through him, I met a lot of important people in the art and literary world... People thought he was a revolutionary.' Rothenstein was quick to defend 'modern art' from those who thought it vulgar.

Moore with Barry Hart, head of stone carving at the RCA, in 1922. Though Moore realized it was important to learn the technical skills of carving by copying classic pieces of European sculpture, he was keen to seek new and unusual sources of inspiration.

London's museums

Moore spent most of his free time at London's many museums and galleries. He went to the National Gallery and Victoria and Albert Museum as well as other museums not directly related to the history of art – the Natural History Museum, the Science Museum and the Geological Museum.

However, his favourite remained the British Museum. He was particularly interested in the history of art, from its prehistoric roots in Palaeolithic art (from the early Stone Age) until, but not including, the

Renaissance. He believed that an artist learns not only by creating art but also by looking at the art of the past. For this reason he turned his back on the contemporary work at the Tate Gallery.

Moore and the modernists

The first decades of the 20th century were a time of incredible artistic development. Technological innovation, science, mass production, war and political change inspired artists to new heights. Traditional art, dance, literature and music witnessed a revolution. **Modernism** – with its rallying cry 'Make it new!' (from a poem by Ezra Pound) – was the name given to these artistic experiments. It provoked enthusiasm and

Mother and Child (1922) by Henry Moore. This 28 cm-high piece showed the influence of Cubism, and also of Mayan and Aztec sculpture from **pre-colonial** Mexico. 'The simple, monumental grandiosity of Aztec sculpture... attracted me enormously,' Moore said later.

Cubism

Cubism took as its starting point Paul Cézanne's belief that all natural forms could be reduced to basic geometrical shapes: cylinders, spheres, cones and blocks. The development of Cubism from around 1907 by Pablo Picasso, Georges Braque and later Juan Gris (see page 58) represented the great break from traditional painting. Cubism attempted to show all four dimensions – height, width, depth and time – in a two dimensional art form. Cubism allowed the examination of an object from a variety of viewpoints, rather than the single viewpoint of traditional painting. This multiple viewpoint implied change or movement and so introduced the idea of the passing of time. Cubism became the most influential artistic movement of the 20th century. It inspired artists in many spheres, and at many levels: from sculpture to literature, from poetry to fashion and ceramic design.

violent outrage. Paris was one of the centres of the modernist revolution and Moore visited the city several times. He was determined to see the paintings by Paul Cézanne (see page 58) that he had read about in Fry's book. In particular, Cézanne's *Bathers* had a profound impact on Moore; though two-dimensional, it seemed to Moore that the figures of the bathers had been sliced from solid rock. He retained an admiration for the *Bathers* paintings until the very end of his life.

In London, the modernist sculptor Henri Gaudier-Brzeska (see page 58) had already made his mark but, like so many young men of his generation, had been killed in his prime in World War I. Moore's sculptural experiments at this time were not completely without precedent, but the directions he subsequently took were very new.

Moore studied at the Royal College of Art until 1924, developing ideas and mastering the skills he needed as a sculptor, craftsman and artist. The direction of his work, however, was heralded in his sculpture *Mother and Child*. Its faceting – the way its different planes and surfaces fitted together – owed a lot to **Cubism**.

Shock of the old

Academic Institutions in the 1920s encouraged budding sculptors to study the **classical figurative** sculpture of the **Renaissance** and the traditions of Ancient Greece. Moore, however, sought other influences and directions. '**Primitive art**, anything other than Greek or imitation Greek, Roman or Italian Renaissance was all thought to be childish... amateur or immature,' Moore said. He visited the British Museum twice a week, and while he diligently studied ancient Greek sculpture, he also pored over specimens from the Pacific Islands, from Africa and, above all, from ancient Mexico. He filled his notebooks with hundreds of sketches of the sculptures he saw, and recorded his thoughts about them.

Moore was stirred by their solidity and simplicity. Like the Spanish painter Picasso, he recognized that primitive art was more 'fundamental' – it was not based on other influences or copied from earlier traditions, but instead the result of genuine, often religious, inspiration. Moved by the massive stone pieces he had seen, Moore became a keen exponent of 'direct carving', where the artist worked directly on the material to create a unique and pure sculpture. He enjoyed the actual physical effort of such work, feeling happier, he said, 'with a chisel and hammer than when using clay'.

A wooden figure of the god Oni, from Nigeria. Ancient sculpture from Africa, Latin America, the Pacific Islands and Europe had a profound effect on many artists in the early decades of the 20th century.

> **"** The European tradition, Moore believed, had made sculpture uninspired and lifeless. *'During the Victorian period, sculpture had become a process whereby the artist would model a figure which was then passed on to workmen to copy... Eric Gill... popularized... direct carving, of doing the whole thing yourself... but the work wasn't very original.'* **"**

The challenge of Italy

In January 1925, Moore won a travelling **scholarship** to Italy. He arrived confidently believing that the Renaissance, like Ancient Greece, was overrated. However, in Florence, Rome and Venice, Moore recognized the majesty and beauty of the works of the great Italian Renaissance artists Michelangelo, Donatello, Masaccio, Titian and Tintoretto. This did huge damage to his conviction that what mattered most was the power in primitive art!

Moore realized the strengths of classical and non-European sculpture had to be united – the problem was how? It caused a 'sculptor's block' for Moore, who couldn't immediately solve the problem. He found it impossible to go on as before or start in a new direction.

Fortune smiled on Moore when the professor of sculpture at the RCA resigned. The government board of education would not let the RCA principal, Rothenstein, appoint the controversial sculptor Jacob Epstein (see page 58) to the post, so Rothenstein put Moore's name forward. Moore was at that time assistant in the sculpture department, and because he was relatively unknown, no objections were raised. He got the job. At a time when he was not selling work and was struggling to come to terms with what he had seen in Italy, this was an opportunity for Moore to develop his own style without having to worry about money.

It also meant he could take his share of family responsibilities. 'I had a tiny place in Hampstead when my mother came to live with me when I had begun to teach then and hated having to leave her alone in the evenings. But she didn't mind, she knew how to rough it. She even did the cooking.'

A new direction

When Moore began sculpting again his pieces showed his efforts to reconcile classical sculpture with non-European art. What he tried to do was identify the ingredients common to both European and primitive art and develop them. According to the art historian and critic John Russell, Moore's first successful sculptures were *Head and Shoulders* and *Torso*, both completed in 1927. Each was 'figurative' – which means that everything in them could be traced back to parts of the human body – but what made them unique was the way the parts were put together.

Sculptures of the human body and of the head and shoulders were essential elements both of the European artistic tradition and of primitive non-European art. Moore combined classical ideas, primitive art and **Cubism**. According to Russell, *Head and Shoulders* was one of the most successful cubist pieces in the world.

Moore finally put everything together with the first of his *Reclining Figures* in 1929. Few themes follow the classical tradition more than the 'reclining figure' – a figure, often of a woman, propped up on one elbow, creating a composition that rises and falls in a continuous line. The reclining figure has been a subject for sculptors and painters for many centuries. It was also common in non-European art, particularly in **pre-colonial** Latin American sculpture.

Head and Shoulders (1927) was one of the first pieces Moore completed that showed the influences of both primitive and classical sculpture.

In his *Reclining Figure* of 1929 Moore used elements of pre-colonial Mexican sculpture and of classical European sculpture. He also included a thick-set sturdiness in his figure that owed a lot to paintings done by Picasso in the early 1920s. Not everyone liked it – the *Daily Mirror* wrote: 'A monstrosity at an exhibition of sculpture by Mr Henry Moore which surpassed in repulsiveness even that of [the sculptor] Epstein.'

Around this time Moore also began to develop an idea that helped make him famous: the human body as a **metaphor** for landscape. In many ways it was not a new idea. Roger Fry, writing about a group of figures by Michelangelo, described them as like a range of mountains viewed from a distance, 'figures so arranged... comparable in breadth and dignity to the mouldings of the earth'. Many famous statues of reclining figures also represented river-goddesses or the spirit of rivers – such as Georg (Raphael) Donner's *The River Ybbs* and Coysevox's *Dordogne*. The power of the human form as a metaphor was also seen in *West Wind*, a decorative **relief** Moore made in 1928–29 for the London Transport headquarters at St James's Park (see page 28).

Reclining Figure, 1929. This piece drew many of Moore's inspirations together. Of particular importance was an ancient Mexican figure called 'Chac-Mool': 'Chac-Mool is the... sculpture that most influenced me in my early work,' he wrote.

The struggle to establish British abstract art

> "
> The critic of the influential London *Morning Post* wrote of Moore's 1928 exhibition: *'Ugliness thrives at the hand of Mr Moore. He shows utter contempt for the natural beauty of women and children.'* Another critic wrote: *'They are grotesque… The women seem… to be suffering from elephantiasis, as well as [other] diseases… they are ugly.'*
> "

The year 1928 was a major turning point in Moore's life and career. He held his first one-man show at the Warren Gallery, London, and several notable sculptors, including Jacob Epstein, bought pieces.

Public abuse...

In trying to develop a new style of sculpture, however, Moore took a lot of critical and personal abuse. During the 1920s and 1930s, the work of **avant-garde** artists attracted a lot of disapproval, ranging from verbal criticism to physical assault. Galleries were unwilling to exhibit them and dealers unwilling to promote them. Work was sometimes judged obscene, but often it was criticized because it did not conform to established **classical** ideas – it was not seen as 'beautiful' and therefore it was not 'art'. Controversial sculptures were even vandalized.

...and private happiness

It was in 1928 that Moore met Irina Radetsky, a painting student of striking appearance. He later called her his most valuable critic. The daughter of a Russian officer, Irina's own life had been dramatic. Born into privilege, her world was turned upside down by World War I and the 1917 **Russian Revolution**. Her father was killed and her mother remarried, but in the turmoil of the Russian Civil War, which followed the Revolution, Irina and her mother were separated. Irina found refuge with her grandmother, who died soon after, and it was several years before Irina was reunited with her mother and stepfather, by then living as exiles in Paris. Educated in England, Irina enrolled as a student at the RCA.

Moore was dazzled by Irina. 'I met her at a dance at the College and more or less took her out for the evening, not realizing she was unofficially engaged... her fiancé, Leslie, was sitting there and I didn't realize he was anything to do with her and ignored him. I walked her back to Kensington Station... Irina and I walking together... and Leslie dragging his feet in the gutter.'

The couple were married in 1929 and stayed in Hampstead. Their social circle included aspiring young artists, architects and writers. However, Moore later claimed, 'My real education was at the British Museum – I did not get anything out of Hampstead – only friends.'

In 1928, several leading sculptors, including Moore and Jacob Epstein, had been asked to provide sculptures to decorate the outside of the new London Transport headquarters above St James's Park Underground station. Moore was **commissioned** to produce a **relief** and the *West Wind* carving was his first effort at monumental public art. Moore was unhappy at the critical public response to the project however, and found commissions too restricting. It was several years before he accepted another one.

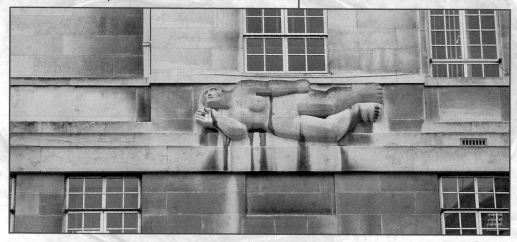

West Wind, by Henry Moore – commissioned by London Transport in 1928 to decorate their new headquarters at St James's Park.

A busy decade

The 1930s were tremendously prolific for Moore: in 1930 alone, he completed 20 carvings. The materials he worked with included **cast** concrete, lead, wood and stone. In 1931 Moore made his first sale to a gallery abroad, and that same year he exhibited three works in the *Plastik* exhibition in Zurich. From that year on, he sought inspiration from a variety of new sources. Moore visited France regularly and was directly influenced by leading artists in Paris, especially Picasso and the sculptors Arp and Giacometti (see page 58). Moore paid Picasso many direct and indirect compliments – his *Reclining Figure* of 1931 owed its open, 'stringed' chest to a **cubist** guitar **motif** used by Picasso.

Britart in the 1930s

Although the 1930s was a decade of **economic depression** and political tension, it also saw a revival in British art. Many **abstract** artists formed clubs such as the Seven and Five Society and Unit One to develop their ideas and support each other against their critics. 'In those days,' wrote Moore, 'modern art had very little following, so people… had to band together to face the opposition.' Moore shared a studio with Barbara Hepworth and Ben Nicholson (see page 58) on Parkhill Road, Hampstead, which gave its name to their circle of artists and writers: The Parkhill Road Group.

Reclining Figure, 1931. Moore continually returned to the theme of the reclining figure. The 1931 figure owed much to Picasso and Cubism.

By now, however, art critics were queuing up to attack his work. Others were supportive, but the tide was against them. The press joined in – one article alleging that as a professor of sculpture, Moore was 'corrupting the young' by making them study his 'monstrosities'. There were demands within the RCA that Moore should be sacked, but Rothenstein stood firm: 'I appointed him for a seven-year period: as this period has not come to an end, he stays.'

In 1932, tired of the ongoing uproar around his employment, Moore resigned. By then he was selling pieces and accepting a few private commissions from discerning art collectors. He was also able to get a job teaching for two days a week at Chelsea School of Art. As his reputation developed, demand for his work grew. He was eventually able to give up teaching to concentrate on sculpture full-time.

Away from the fray

Moore's favourite subject remained the female form. He reduced the human figure to its simplest and most '**organic**' elements – legs, arms, chest, breasts, head – and moved away from the **figurative**

Reclining Figure, 1937. The smoothly flowing and elongated lines of this *Reclining Figure* show the growing influence of Surrealism on Moore's work.

towards abstract, almost alien shapes. They were not to everyone's taste: when a friend bought a sculpture and put it in his front garden in Hampstead, the neighbours complained!

At his country cottage at Kingston, Kent, Moore kept up an exhausting routine of work, stimulated and inspired by the natural environment. At the nearby resort of Broadstairs, he collected bags full of sea pebbles, flints and bones – 'nature's sculpture' he called them. These he would work into what he called **'found-and-altered'** pieces – objects removed from their natural setting and built into sculptures. At Shakespeare Cliff he carved the chalk. 'It was around this time that Bernard Meadows began to help me… we would get up at six o'clock, throw a bucket of water over each other, have breakfast, and then work until eleven. Irina would make sandwiches and we'd all go to Shakespeare Cliff to bathe and picnic. We'd get back by one and work until dark. After supper, I would draw until eleven or twelve. This was a regular routine… I am amazed… at how much work was done then.'

Holidays at the Norfolk coast were more restful: 'I would just take a piece of stone and carve it on the beach – any beach would have suited me.'

> **"** *'I remember going to a surrealist meeting at which Salvador Dali [see page 58] was the speaker. We all sat there for 25 minutes or so and nothing happened, just an empty stage. Everyone was getting fed up... when suddenly there was an enormous bang and a great puff of smoke and, as it cleared, there was Dali in a diver's suit and diver's helmet.'* **"**
> Henry Moore, 1985

By the late 1930s, landscape, especially the undulations of the English landscape – its hills, valleys and moors – had become a principal inspiration. His work began to feature holes carved through the stone: 'A hole can have as much meaning as a solid mass – there is a mystery in a hole in a cliff or hillside, in its depth and shape... I was trying to make the sculpture as fully realized as nature.'

The politics of art

Although Moore had joined the Seven and Five Society and Unit One, groups that promoted modern art and architecture in a political way (see box page 28) he was not 'political' in his art. He believed politics had very little to do with art. However, his critics in the press had other ideas: they expressed hatred of his art by labelling it **'Bolshevist'** because it was revolutionary and challenging.

Moore was, however, very sympathetic to the **surrealist** movement. Surrealism challenged realism with humour, dream and absurdity. Moore's found-and-altered objects were his most surreal pieces and, in 1936, he contributed to surrealist exhibitions in London and New York.

Moore's political beliefs, like his father's, were **radical**. After a visit with Irina to Spain in 1934, he became a passionate defender of the Spanish Republic. Moore was part of a group of artists who tried to aid the Republican cause during the **Spanish Civil War** of 1936–39. He and others campaigned to end the British government's policy of non-intervention – that is of not becoming involved in the conflict. **Nazi** Germany and **Fascist** Italy were openly aiding the Spanish rebels led by General Franco. Moore, like many people in Britain and Europe, believed that Britain's non-intervention was wrong because the Spanish government was a legitimate, elected body. Failing to challenge Nazi **expansionism** would inevitably lead to a second world war.

World War II

World War II began with the German invasion of Poland on
1 September 1939. Two days later Britain and France declared war on
Germany. During the so-called 'phoney war' there were no hostilities
for six months: a **blackout** was implemented, gas masks were issued
and air raid defences prepared. But for many, life carried on as
normal. Hostilities started in earnest in April 1940 and soon prevented
Moore from teaching. A shortage of available stone also stopped any
large-scale sculpting. The war had an even more direct impact on
Moore: his London home was bombed, though luckily neither he nor
Irina were at home at the time. They moved to Hoglands, a former pig
farm in Perry Green, Hertfordshire, north of London. It remained their
home for the rest of their lives.

The *Shelter Drawings*

In autumn 1940 Moore began work as an **official war artist**. He
had always been a prolific sketcher and drawing continued to be an
important part of his artistic studies. Today his best-known drawings
remain the *Shelter Drawings*.

As a subject, London's Underground shelters matched Moore's interest
in caves and underground imagery. He was dumbfounded by the sight
of thousands of people lying helpless in the dark while violence was

London's air raid shelters

In preparation for an invasion of Britain, the German air force
(*Luftwaffe*) launched what became known as the **Blitz** – a
bombing campaign aimed at major cities, intended to terrorize
the country into surrender. Because the *Luftwaffe* targeted
populated areas, shelter became a priority. The London
Underground, with its complex network of tunnels and
subterranean platforms, offered a ready-made solution. Tens
of thousands of people found sanctuary night after night,
crowded together on the dark, claustrophobic platforms.

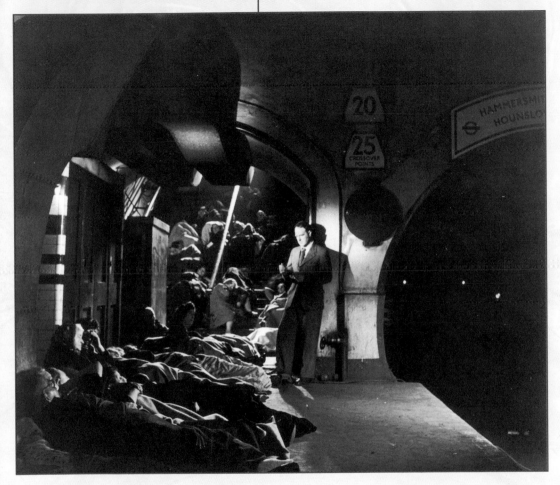

committed to their homes, factories and neighbourhoods above. 'I had never seen so many reclining figures... Amid the grim tension, I noticed... strangers formed together in intimate groups and children asleep within feet of the passing trains.'

The figures he portrayed were like corpses already wrapped in their shrouds. The jumble of bodies seemed to foreshadow the horrors of the **Nazi** death-camps, at that time impossible to imagine. But despite the hardship they portrayed, the drawings also lent nobility to the people's suffering.

Moore also sketched coalminers at work, reminding people that conflicts were not won solely by men with guns but by everyone working for the common cause. He chose a pit near Castleford where his own father had worked as a miner years before. The conditions, he said, were the closest thing he could imagine to hell.

> *'With the Shelter Drawings, Moore became… one of the keepers of the public conscience. People were persuaded… that a dogged grandeur attached to the life they were leading. The squalid elements… dropped away, and what remained behind was on the scale of epic.'*
> John Russell, art historian and critic

Madonna and Child

Moore had not done any large-scale sculpture for some time, but in 1943 the Reverend Walter Hussey, a clergyman with a **radical** taste for art, **commissioned** him to carve a Madonna and Child for St Matthew's Church, Northampton. 'Religious art has been the inspiration for the greatest works of art in the world,' Moore later wrote. 'The Mother and Child... has been a universal theme from the beginning of time and some of the earliest sculptures... from the Neolithic Age are of a mother and child. With the Madonna and Child, there was the religious element too... Nor did I want to create something the average person would find dreadful or wrong.' *Madonna and Child* would be a masterpiece that subtly combined all the elements of his life's work so far – **pre-colonial** American and African sculpture, the religious figures of the **Renaissance** and **classical** sculpture – and hinted at his future direction.

Moore's *Madonna and Child*, St Matthew's Church, Northampton. Many were astonished that an **avant-garde** sculptor like Moore could produce a piece with such immediate appeal. In fact it embodied all his major influences.

In St Matthew's Church, the *Madonna and Child* was positioned directly opposite a dramatic crucifixion scene painted by Moore's friend and contemporary, the British **abstract** artist Graham Sutherland.

35

Fame and a family

By 1945 Moore was one of the most famous artists in the world. Honoured throughout the UK, he was made a **trustee** of the Tate Gallery in London, a member of the Arts Council's art panel and an honorary doctor of literature at the University of Leeds. When he went to Paris in November 1945, it was, according to art critic and historian John Russell, 'almost as an official visitor'. In 1946 he made his first trip to New York, where the Museum of Modern Art gave him a major **retrospective** exhibition. Soon there were more retrospectives and honours.

The honours counted little to Moore. Confident and straightforward in his tastes, he had been on personal terms with the nine or ten other people who really counted in the realm of **avant-garde** sculpture since the 1930s, including the famous Spanish artist Picasso. Moore held Picasso in very high regard: 'Picasso and the British Museum were the only sources that I ever really needed.'

The art that first endeared Moore to the British public was his most recognizably **figurative** and humane – the *Shelter Drawings* and his *Madonna and Child*. His more characteristic work of the late 1940s and 1950s became popular because it seemed to capture the same progressive post-war spirit that ushered in the **welfare state**. The welfare state was the government-led effort to eradicate poverty and unemployment after the war by introducing a free National Health Service, affordable housing and new pension and unemployment benefits.

Until he was 50 Moore earned little more than the average schoolteacher, but by the late 1940s he was an international figure and his earnings increased.

A new opportunity

In 1945, people throughout Europe emerged from the horrors of total war. Peace was a cause for celebration: a time to look forward, a time of faith, a time to embrace progress and the brave new world. The thoroughly modern sculptures of Henry Moore, along with those of

Epstein and Hepworth, now seemed to epitomize the new spirit. Moore was promoted by the British Council as an artistic ambassador for these new times. His work portrayed the same kind of 'can-do' optimism that made the 1948 London Olympics and the 1951 **Festival of Britain** so successful.

Housing developments and entire 'New Towns', such as Stevenage in Hertfordshire, were built. These not only re-housed people who had lost homes in the **Blitz**, but also replaced the slums that had blighted urban life before the war. It is no accident that Moore's sculptures grace many of these grand schemes.

Henry and Irina stayed on at Hoglands, slowly developing the house and its surroundings. They added a sitting room, increased the number of studios and extended the garden in order to display Moore's sculptures. The house also became home to Moore's growing collection of pieces by other artists, including pictures by Ruskin, Seurat, Picasso, Degas, Rodin, Cézanne and Goya. He also built up a collection of sculpture from all ages and civilizations.

Henry Moore's *King and Queen*. This regal couple serenely survey their realm – the beautiful valley of Glenkiln, Scotland. Moore called it the most perfect setting for his sculpture.

In 1946 Irina gave birth to a daughter. They named her Mary after Moore's mother and his sister – with perhaps a nod to the Madonna. Henry, Irina and Mary enjoyed their privacy at Hoglands while adapting to a new way of life. Now a proud father, Moore allowed the image of the family to dominate his work until the end of the 1940s. Irina dutifully looked after Henry while he adapted to the change of life.

The influence of family life crept into his work in other ways too. By the time Mary was six, she enjoyed having Henry read bedtime stories to her. Many of these fairy stories featured kings and queens which gave inspiration for one of Moore's most famous sculpures, *King and Queen*.

Truth to material

Until the 1940s, Moore had believed that sculptors should show 'truth to material'. This meant that artists should let the material they work with help them shape their sculpture and also acknowledge that every material has limits. He used the example of carving a heavy stone figure with very thin ankles: it would simply break during the making. Moore did not like the devices used by **classical** sculptors – for example, modelling a tree trunk or some other disguised brace up the back of one leg in order to support the figure. Instead, he believed, the material should have its say: 'a thing in wood has qualities of its own, as thin as the branch of a tree, which stone can't be'.

By the late 1940s this idea had become a restraint. After the war, Moore's work was principally **cast** in bronze. Bronze allowed for an increase in size, and Moore began increasingly to work on a monumental scale. Many of his monumental bronzes were exhibited throughout the world, further enhancing his fame and reputation. In using bronze, which is essentially a copying material, Moore could create a full-sized model in a wide range of materials, before making moulds and casting it in bronze. There is no 'truth' in bronze, he said: bronze can be anything.

Helmet heads and warriors

Signs of Moore's next phase were already apparent. In the 1940s he began to experiment with what he called 'helmet heads'. He revisited this theme, creating surreal helmeted heads that resembled knights – the warriors of the old dark ages – as well as pilots of nuclear bombers – the warriors of the new dark ages.

Helmet Head No 2, 1950. By the late 1940s, Moore's preoccupation with the theme of war and peace was obvious in many of his sculptures.

Moore's attitude to war was now very different to that of the youthful, enthusiastic combatant he had been in World War I. The rules, he knew, had changed. The mechanized carnage of 1914–18 had been appalling but had seemed to obey some rules. World War II had been a very different conflict – from its merciless bombing of civilians and slaughter of Jews, Russians, Poles, gypsies and homosexuals to the radioactive horrors of the atomic raids on Hiroshima and Nagasaki in Japan.

Moore's helmet heads, both menacing and protective, were part of his sculptural response to the war and the dawning of the atomic age. Soon he was creating dismembered, fallen warriors lying beside their shields. In 1953–54, Moore completed a dramatic statue as a memorial for the dead of Arnhem, the scene of a World War II military disaster.

As was often the case, Moore had many sources of inspiration. He remembered 'a pebble I found on the sea-shore. It reminded me of a stump of a leg amputated at the hip.' There were also the broken statues of Greek warriors in museums. In their helpless heroism, these mutilated soldiers echoed the pitiful old veterans of World War I.

Warrior with Shield, 1954, depicted a pathetic warrior, arm and leg severed, raising his shield as if to ward off the final killing blow.

Moore's so-called 'Greek period', in which he worked almost exclusively in bronze, also saw him casting the figures of **draped** women. These draped figures became almost as popular as the *Shelter Drawings*, and it was the figures of those sheltering, Moore claimed, that convinced him to experiment with the use of draperies. After visiting Greece in 1951, he said, 'Drapery can emphasize the tension in a figure... pulled tight across the form... [in] contrast with the crumpled slackness between.'

Like his Italian visit of 1924, the visit to Greece had its share of artistic revelations. Moore also saw in drapery connections to landscape, comparing the draperies to the folds of hills, valleys and mountains: 'the crinkled skin of the earth'.

Another important theme in Moore's work was his *Internal/External Forms*, composed of two shapes, one enclosing the other, like giant versions of the helmet heads. A German writer at the time saw these as like a mother carrying the child inside herself, or like the Egyptian coffins that symbolize the mother goddess holding the dead Pharaoh like a child again. However, other writers noticed that the figures were similar to hollow trees – and many such trees stood on the boundaries of Henry and Irina's home in Hertfordshire.

The Time-Life figures

Soon after his return from Greece, Henry was **commissioned** by the architects of the new Time-Life building in London to produce a sculpture and screen. The sculpture was another reclining female figure, draped in a way that clearly suggested the folds of the earth as if viewed from space. The screen could be seen from both the street and the courtyard containing the reclining figure.

The screen – 8 metres in length and almost 3 metres high – was made of four parts. Moore's intention was to make each element movable to allow periodic variation. Unfortunately health and safety regulations stopped this. Moore was unhappy with the final position, high above a narrow street and difficult to see. He later said that he would give a great deal to take the screen away and make use of the ideas 'imprisoned within it'.

Time-Life Screen, 1952–53. Though the Time-Life commission did not work out as Moore had hoped, others considered it a great success.

41

> "
> After his experience with the Time-Life building, Moore remained in two minds about the relationship between sculptors and architects. He certainly did not agree that architecture was the 'mother of the arts'. *'Painting and sculpture existed long before architecture... In Palaeolithic times, men lived in caves... yet painting and sculpture were already going strong.'*
> "

Between 1955 and 1960, Moore received further accolades: he was made a member of the Order of the Companions of Honour, and a **trustee** of the National Gallery in London. In 1956, he was invited to Holland, to mark the 350th anniversary of Rembrandt's birth.

Moore continued to complete **commissions** for architects and designers, including free-standing sculptures and wall **reliefs**. The reliefs were composed of both **organic** and machine parts – vertebrae, leg-bones, screw heads, valves, shells. Looking like the incomprehensible controls of alien spacecraft, they were reminiscent of his **surrealist** phase of the 1930s.

Moore's 'motives'

Cast in bronze or hewn from stone, Moore's upright figures were often lean and sinuous. Moore followed the standing figures with totem pole-like **'motives'**. Asked to provide a piece to go in front of a new building in Italy, he visited the site and noticed a lone Lombardy poplar tree growing nearby. It convinced him that a vertical figure would counterbalance the low, horizontal lines of the building. 'Back home in

---

Bronze-casting

Bronze-casting allows an artist to make more than one cast of a piece of work. 'If you make a mould,' Moore said, '...you could make 30 – even 100 – as good as each other.' Dealers often asked Moore to make several casts. He was happy to do a small run, but not too many: 'numbers make something... less unique'.

England... I started by balancing different forms one above the other, with results rather like the northwest American totem-poles.'

Though Moore rejected the Italian commission when he discovered the sculpture would be sited in a car park, he continued the theme. His models became more organic or 'biomorphic' – resembling living growing forms. Ancient sites such as Stonehenge in England or the standing stones of Brittany, France exert an almost primal power over the imagination: Moore's upright motives had a similar impact. 'One... took the shape of a crucifix: a kind of worn-down body and a cross merged into one.' This became the *Glenkiln Cross*, which stands in Glenkiln, Scotland, a place Moore described as 'the most perfect setting for sculpture... I'd sooner have my sculptures surrounded by natural landscape... than with man-made architecture.'

Three Upright Motives (including the *Glenkiln Cross*). The religious meaning of the arrangement – suggesting the three crosses on the hill at Golgotha – only came to Moore when he was arranging the maquettes.

Moore set a cast of the *Glenkiln Cross* on a pedestal between two other free-standing motives in an arrangement that suggested a religious meaning. 'When I came to carry out some of [the] **maquettes** in their final size, three of them grouped themselves together and, in my mind, assumed the aspect of a crucifixion scene, as though framed in the sky above Golgotha.'

A gentler pace

Henry was now in his mid-fifties. To help him cope with the increasing size of his work he employed several assistants, some of whom became sculptors in their own right including Anthony Caro and Phillip King. His youthful enthusiasm for rising at dawn and shocking himself awake with cold water had given way to a more domesticated arrangement: 'I try to be in the studio by 9.30 and I try to have no interruptions in the mornings... up to teatime I'm quite resigned now that the afternoons aren't for proper work. But... I like to go back to the studio from about six.'

The UNESCO commission

Despite the fear public bodies had of such an irrepressible imagination, Moore attracted very prestigious commissions. He was asked to provide a piece to stand outside the new headquarters of

Reclining Figure, 1958 – UNESCO Building, Paris, France. It was cheaper for Moore to travel and work where the stone was cut in Italy than have it transported to England.

> **"** *'The UNESCO sculpture was to be so big that the cost of sending the stone to England would have swallowed up the whole of my fee,'* Moore said. It was cheaper to travel to the stone! *'I was in Italy intermittently for nearly a year. I would go over for three or four weeks, work on the stone and, because I hated being away from Irina and Mary... I would come home for a month and then go back again.'* **"**

UNESCO (the United Nations Educational, Scientific and Cultural Organization) in Paris. UNESCO was established in 1946 to promote collaboration between nations and people through education, science and culture. Picasso and Joan Miró (see page 58) were also involved with the organization.

Moore rejected several themes, such as mothers and children, and family groups, that were loosely related to UNESCO's aspirations. In the end, he chose to revisit his *Reclining Figures*. In 1958 he completed *Reclining Figure* in Roman travertine marble for the site. It was over 5 metres in length. Moore's only criticism of the UNESCO project was the building, which fuelled his suspicion that architects only think of embellishing their buildings as an afterthought.

A few years later, when Moore was awarded the Feltrinelli Prize in Italy – and $42,000 – he and Irina bought a holiday cottage and studio close to the marble quarry where he worked on *Reclining Figure*, in the coastal town of Forte dei Marmi.

Moore and marble

Easy to carve and polish, marble has attracted sculptors for thousands of years. The best marble in the world comes from the Carrara Mountains in Italy. What excited Moore about working with marble was his sense of continuity: the quarry where he chose his stone was the same quarry in which Michelangelo had worked centuries before. He also took childish pleasure in the sheer scale of the quarrying operation, the workers like ants on the quarry-side, the solid blocks as big as houses manoeuvred down the mountainside.

The 1960s

The 1960s were a time of change, excitement and optimism. In art, music and science, Britain seemed to lead the world. Prime Minister Harold Wilson talked of the 'white-heat' of the technological revolution. Henry Moore again seemed to capture the spirit of the times in his work. Now in his sixties, Moore was also an icon for post-war Britain, honoured by bodies in Britain, Italy, the USA, Germany and Canada.

Fame and fortune

Moore was now a wealthy man and one of the most sought-after sculptors in the world. This meant he could develop his art free of economic constraints. One commentator thought it possible to plot on a graph a direct relationship between Moore's income and the size of his work! The only limitations on his sculptures now were the dimensions of his studios and the weight that lorries could carry. 'At one time I became interested in doing my own **casting**… so I built a little foundry at the bottom of the garden,' Moore said. 'Now I send all my sculptures to London for the medium- and life-size ones… [and] Berlin for the really big ones.'

New work and new directions

Moore continued to receive **commissions** from organizations as varied as the San Francisco Longshoremen's Union and Yale University. Artistically, he began to explore shapes inspired by **organic** life, the human body, bones and their function – pieces that look like the working elements of joints, shoulder blades and kneecaps.

In 1961, Moore was asked to provide a sculpture for the Lincoln Center in New York. The proposed location was in the middle of a pool

---

Moore and money
Moore maintained many unaffected qualities, playing table tennis with Mary, enjoying a bottle of ale with his lunch. When guests came, the only obvious concessions to his wealth were small silver plates under each bottle of beer!

of water and he was excited by the possibilities of relating a large work to the ever-shifting surface.

The finished sculpture was another reclining figure, this time split into two massive, bony parts. Cast in bronze and 8 metres long and over 4 metres high, it was twice the size of the UNESCO form. Before making the full-size plaster model, Moore and his assistants first had to construct a huge shelter of polythene over metal scaffolding.

Another important sculpture of the period is the *Knife Edge Two Piece* (1962–65). A cast of this stands outside the Houses of Parliament in London.

Knife Edge Two Piece, 1962–65. Standing outside the Houses of Parliament, this sculpture has become a familiar backdrop for television interviews with British politicians.

47

In 1966 Moore completed *Atom Piece* for the University of Chicago. It was here that the Italian physicist Enrico Fermi first experimented with the controlled release of nuclear power. Based on an elephant skull, *Atom Piece* looms like the mushroom cloud of an atomic explosion. That same year he also completed *Double Oval* in bronze: a pair of dramatically holed and streamlined oval shapes.

Another of Moore's successful bone structures was *The Arch*, built in various sizes and materials between 1962 and 1969. The largest, of bronze, stands over 4.7 metres high. At a **retrospective** of Moore's work in Florence, Italy, *The Arch* became a local landmark – every day, young bridal couples came to be photographed standing beneath it! Moore also finished *Three Piece Sculpture: Vertebrae* in 1969. Though based on the natural shapes of vertebrae, it was enlarged to become a very **abstract** piece. A larger version, *Three Forms Vertebrae*, also known as *The Dallas Piece*, now stands outside Dallas City Hall, Texas.

Although Moore continued to draw throughout his life, by this stage he had stopped using drawings as a way of planning sculpture: he felt that in many ways they limited his imagination. In the early 1970s, however, he developed an interest in printmaking. Using a combination of new and old techniques, he produced etchings and **lithographs** of landscapes, seascapes, figures and a famous series of sheep.

A full-scale model of *The Arch* under construction at Hoglands, prior to casting in bronze.

Hoglands

Over the years Moore bought up land surrounding Hoglands. As the estate grew, he had to resort to a bicycle to get from one studio to another. Buildings were added to house the growing archives containing his sketches, drawings, prints and etchings and his tools and materials.

In 1970 the Bourne **Maquette** Studio was built to house Moore's accumulation of plasters, terracotta pieces and 'found objects'. One room was used for making and displaying maquettes and a second floor for enlarging them to medium-sized plasters called 'working models'. Eventually the Hoglands estate occupied over 28 hectares.

New critics

Inevitably, any successful person is open to resentment from others. There had always been those ready to deride Moore's work, but towards the end of the 1960s, as his international reputation blossomed, his standing amongst many artists in Britain slipped. A new generation questioned the validity of his work, just as he had challenged the validity of the **classical** and **Renaissance** period. Some argued that the increasing size of his works, his increasing reliance on bronze and his relatively narrow range of subjects demonstrated that his imaginative powers were limited. Some claimed his growing popularity and his promotion by British arts bodies had affected the quality and artistic purity seen in his early works. Others reacted to the adulation he received, alleging he had 'sold out' and become a man of the establishment – conveniently forgetting that he had turned down a knighthood in the 1950s. Even friendly critics disapproved of the practice of casting early Moore carvings in bronze, or manufacturing larger replicas of the originals: 'Conditions in which it would be very easy for an artist to turn into a one-man souvenir shop,' as John Russell wrote.

However, Moore kept his views to himself. Although he continued to enjoy the company of others, artistically he became more introverted – a private artist in the most public of media.

The 1970s and 1980s

Henry Moore was by now not simply the creator of Britain's most public art, but was also becoming Britain's most public artist. Film crews, photographers and journalists watched him work; parties were shown round his studio. The Moores had always been happy to oblige visitors, but as the numbers of artists, collectors, students and young people grew they realized a system had to be established. There was also a growing demand that the Hoglands collection should be properly displayed, and a fear about what might happen to the collection after Moore's death.

The Henry Moore Foundation

Moore spent a lot of time in the 1970s cementing his reputation and ensuring that his work would benefit others in years to come. In 1972,

Henry Moore and the Queen at the opening of the Henry Moore Sculpture Gallery, Leeds, in 1982.

he established the Henry Moore Trust, to prevent his collection being dispersed to pay **death duties**. The Henry Moore Foundation was registered as a charity in 1977, with Irina and Mary as its **trustees**. Moore gave the Hoglands estate – its studios, houses, archives and collection of work – to the trustees to preserve his work and reputation and to assist the arts in general and sculpture in particular. In 1980 Moore laid the foundation stone for the Henry Moore Institute in Leeds, endowed by the Henry Moore Foundation.

The final years

Meanwhile, his work enjoyed a rich final flourish. In the 1970s, he returned to basic **motifs** with a different and more sharp, edgy quality. Figures turned in upon each other to prick and penetrate larger forms. The flocks of sheep around Hoglands inspired his famous monumental sculpture *Sheep Piece* in 1972.

Sheep Piece, 1972. One of the many playful and humorous sculptures inspired by the immediate environment of Hoglands.

At the same time, his earlier work was reaching a greater audience. In 1972, at Forte di Belvedere (a fort designed by Michelangelo on the edge of Florence, Italy) there was a major **retrospective** of Moore's work, showing 289 exhibits. The ramparts of the fort were a perfect setting for his work. A total of 345,000 visitors came to see them during the four and a half months the show was open. Closure was held back by a week so that Moore could show the then British Prime Minister Edward Heath round personally.

In 1977, Paris also staged an enormous retrospective. In 1978, to mark Moore's 80th birthday, there was an exhibition at the Serpentine Gallery, in London's Kensington Gardens.

By the end of the 1970s there were an average of 40 exhibitions a year, from the very small to dealers' shows and touring exhibitions around the world, organized by the British Council. In 1981 the Madrid exhibition of his work was the first major foreign exhibition in Spain – a country he had loved since visiting in 1934 – for over 40 years. It marked the end of the dictatorship of General Franco and

Henry Moore at work in his maquette studio which, in old age, became the centre of his artistic activity.

Spain's return to the cultural life of Europe. Unfortunately Moore was not well enough to travel to the show, which proved immensely popular and attracted 10,000 visitors in the first weekend. There were other retrospectives, at the Metropolitan Museum in New York in 1983 and in Hong Kong and Japan in 1986.

In his final years, public and politicians honoured Moore. Both German Chancellor Helmut Schmidt and, later, French President François Mitterrand flew to Hoglands by helicopter to present awards. Meanwhile, Moore was giving back. He made a gift of 200 sculptures and drawings and a complete collection of **graphics** to the Art Gallery of Ontario; another 30 major pieces and another collection of graphics went to the Tate Gallery, London. Drawings were given to the British Museum, graphics to the Victoria and Albert Museum and the British Council. The Henry Moore Foundation collection includes over 600 sculptures, 400 original plasters, 3000 drawings, 30 sketchbooks and almost 8000 **lithographs** and etchings.

In his old age, the small **maquette** studio became the centre of Moore's working life, while his assistants worked up the full-sized pieces from his models. Only illness could keep him away. He spent time reworking bronze figures based on Cézanne's *Bathers* paintings, and towards the end of his life he was planning an underground sculpture. It would be a maze, inspired by childhood games in a warren of tunnels near his Castleford home, where children could crawl with only a reel of cotton to guide them back out. As he grew older, he asked to be taken for a drive every day to refresh his vision, his memories and his senses.

Henry Moore died at home, aged 88, on 31 August 1986.

The legacy of Henry Moore

Henry Moore succeeded in creating a new language of sculpture. He drew together sources of inspiration from all ages and continents to create a dynamic and unmistakable style of his own. He quickly established himself as the greatest sculptor of his age, becoming a major influence on his fellows and inspiring generations of artists. He realized that so much beautiful sculpture had been ignored or had been forgotten, overshadowed by **classical** sculpture. He recognized the profound quality of Latin American and African art, learned from it, adapted and transformed it. With a small number of contemporaries, he revived sculpture as an artistic medium.

Some commentators deny Moore was ever an **abstract** artist. In some ways they are correct: Moore took recognizable human and animal forms and worked them into abstraction, rather than creating purely abstract forms.

Henry Moore, photographed in 1967, in one of the marble quarries of the Carrara Mountains in Italy.

Moore's very 'ordinariness' — his composed and unpretentious character — was as solid as one of his own sculptures. As a man, he enjoyed a domestic orderliness with Irina and daughter Mary that enabled him to create a centre of artistic activity at Hoglands.

Moore established relationships with an entire generation of British artists who were often overshadowed by their more extrovert European contemporaries. He suffered critical abuse in his early career, including the loss of his post at the RCA, and it was the very human *Shelter Drawings* that first endeared him to the British people. Yet Moore remained very patient and tolerant — proud of his Yorkshire heritage and his **working-class** roots. He was able to cope with years of criticism and a popular hostility that was whipped up by the press. He seemed to appreciate, if not sympathize with, the suspicion many ordinary people have of modern art.

Moore can also be seen as a direct descendant of the medieval carvers whose work he had admired as a young boy. Although his work did not set out to be religious, it struck a deep chord within ordinary people. Completing the *Madonna and Child*, he recognized that his work had to speak to the many, and that he had to modify his own **radical** artistic vision to that end.

Despite the honours heaped upon him, Henry Moore remains more highly regarded abroad than in the land of his birth. However, at a 1999 celebration at the Yale Center for British Art in the USA, Henry Moore was acclaimed as a 20th century heir to Michelangelo and the sculptors of the ancient world. In 2000, a tour of China organized by the British Council and the Henry Moore Foundation introduced his work to a new and immensely enthusiastic audience. And in 2001, 'Sculpting the 20th Century', the first major US **retrospective** for 20 years, opened in Dallas, Texas.

Henry Moore's reputation as an artist continues to grow, and his influence on modern art in the present century looks set to be as important as his influence on the last.

Timeline

1898	Born 30 July in Castleford, Yorkshire.
1910	Wins a **scholarship** to Castleford Secondary School.
1915–16	Works as a **student teacher**.
1917	Enlists in the army and is gassed at the Battle of Cambrai.
1919–21	Studies at the Leeds College of Art.
1921–24	Studies at the Royal College of Art, London.
1922	*Mother and Child*.
1925	Travels on a scholarship to Italy.
1925–32	Teaches at the Royal College of Art, London.
1927	*Head and Shoulders*.
1928	Has first solo exhibition, at the Warren Gallery, London.
1929	Marries Irina Radetsky. Completes *Masks*, his first *Reclining Figure* and *West Wind* relief for the headquarters of London Transport.
1931	Has one-man show at the Leicester Galleries, London. Epstein writes introduction to catalogue. First sale to a gallery abroad.
1931–39	First important series of *Reclining Figures*.
1932	Moore returns to mother and child theme. Resigns from RCA.
1932–39	Teaches at Chelsea School of Art.
1934	Contributes to Unit One exhibition. Visits Spain.
1936	Campaigns against Britain's non-intervention in the **Spanish Civil War**. Participates in the first **surrealist** exhibition in the UK.
1939	Outbreak of World War II.
1940	Moves with Irina to Hoglands. Travels to London as an **official war artist** and makes the *Shelter Drawings*.
1942	Returns to Castleford to draw coalminers at work.
1943	First solo exhibition in New York, at the Buchholz Gallery. **Commissioned** to make *Madonna and Child* for a church in Northampton.
1945	End of World War II.
1946	Birth of daughter, Mary. **Retrospective** exhibition presented by The Museum of Modern Art, New York.

1948	Awarded the International Prize for Sculpture at the Venice Biennale.
1948–49	*Family Group.*
1950	*Helmet Head No 2.*
1951	Retrospective exhibition presented by the Tate Gallery, London. Moore's first visit to Greece. *Reclining Figure: Festival* exhibited at the **Festival of Britain**.
1952–53	*Draped Reclining Figure* and *Time-Life Screen* unveiled at the Time-Life building, Bond Street, London.
1953–56	*Warrior Figures. Internal/External Forms.*
1955–56	*Upright Motives*, including the *Glenkiln Cross.*
1956	Commissioned to make a sculpture for the new UNESCO headquarters in Paris.
1958	Completes *Reclining Figure* (UNESCO sculpture).
1961	Elected member of the American Academy and Institute of Arts and Letters, New York. Commissioned to provide a piece for the Lincoln Center, New York.
1962	Begins *The Arch* series and *Knife Edge Two Piece.*
1963	Moore is awarded the Antonio Feltrinelli Prize for Sculpture in Rome.
1965	*Reclining Figure* unveiled at Lincoln Center, New York.
1966	Completes *Atom Piece* for the University of Chicago.
1968	Exhibition in honour of Moore's 70th birthday at the Tate Gallery, London.
1971–72	*Sheep Piece* series.
1972	345,000 people visit the major retrospective exhibition at Forte di Belvedere, Florence.
1977	Establishes the Henry Moore Foundation in Much Hadham, Hertfordshire.
1978	Exhibitions in honour of Moore's 80th birthday at the Serpentine Gallery, London and City Art Gallery, Bradford. Bronze interpretation of Cézanne's *Bathers.*
1982	Henry Moore Sculpture Gallery, Leeds, opened by the Queen.
1983	Exhibition at the Metropolitan Museum of Art, New York.
1986	Dies 31 August in Hertfordshire.

Key artists of Moore's time

Arp, Jean (also known as Hans Arp) (1887–1966). French sculptor, painter and poet. One of the founders of Dadaism – that later developed into Surrealism. Later developed organic abstract sculpture based on natural forms.

Brancusi, Constantin (1876–1957). Romanian abstract artist and sculptor.

Braque, Georges (1882–1963). Painter and founder with Picasso of Cubism.

Cézanne, Paul (1839–1906). Post-impressionist painter, forerunner of the cubist movement.

Dali, Salvador (1904–89). Spanish surrealist artist, writer, poet.

Degas, Edgar (1834–1917). French Impressionist painter and sculptor.

Epstein, Jacob (1880–1959). American who moved to Britain in 1905. Controversial pioneer of Symbolic sculpture.

Gaudier-Brzeska, Henri (1891–1915). Pioneering French modernist sculptor, who died in World War I.

Giacometti, Alberto (1901–66). Swiss sculptor and painter. Joined the surrealists in 1930 and produced many abstract sculptures.

Gill, Eric (1882–1940). Controversial English painter, carver, sculptor.

Gris, Juan (pseudonym of José Victoriano González) (1887–1927). Painter and sculptor and an important participant in the development of Cubism.

Hepworth, Barbara (1903–75). One of the greatest sculptors of the 20th century. She and Moore developed a long artistic association and friendship.

Miró, Joan (1893–1983). Surrealist artist born in Barcelona, Spain. Spent most of his life in France.

Nicholson, Ben (1894–1982). Largely self-taught English abstract artist. Barbara Hepworth was his second wife.

Picasso, Pablo (1881–1973). Spanish artist, the dominant figure in 20th-century art.

Rodin, Auguste (1840–1917). French sculptor chiefly concerned with the human form in his work.

Ruskin, John (1819–1900). Writer, art critic and watercolourist, influential voice on British art.

Major collections

Henry Moore was extremely prolific. His work can be seen in many public places. Collections can be seen in museums and art galleries around the world. They include:

Albright-Knox Art Gallery, Buffalo, New York, USA

Art Gallery of New South Wales, Sydney, Australia

The Art Gallery of Ontario, Toronto, Canada

The Art Institute of Chicago, Chicago, Illinois, USA

Arts Council of Great Britain, London, UK

Auckland City Art Gallery, Auckland, New Zealand

The Baltimore Museum of Art, Baltimore, Maryland, USA

City Art Gallery, Manchester, UK

The Cleveland Museum of Art, Cleveland, Ohio, USA

Contemporary Art Museum, Hiroshima, Japan

Dallas Museum of Art, Dallas, Texas, USA

Fogg Art Museum, Harvard University, Cambridge, Massachusetts, USA

Leeds City Art Gallery, Leeds, UK

Montreal Museum of Fine Arts, Montreal, Canada

Museo Nacional Centro de Arte Reina Sofía, Madrid, Spain

The Museum of Modern Art, New York, USA

National Gallery of Art, Washington DC, USA

National Gallery of Victoria, Melbourne, Australia

Nationalgalerie, Berlin, Germany

Peggy Guggenheim Collection, Venice, Italy

Philadelphia Museum of Art, Philadelphia, Pennsylvania, USA

Rijksmuseum Kröller-Müller, Otterlo, Netherlands

The Saint Louis Art Museum, Saint Louis, Missouri, USA

San Francisco Museum of Modern Art, San Francisco, California, USA

Scottish National Gallery of Modern Art, Edinburgh, UK

Stedelijk Museum, Amsterdam, Netherlands

Tate Gallery, London, UK

Wakefield Art Gallery and Wakefield Museum, Wakefield, UK

Glossary

abstract art in which there is no attempt to represent people or objects realistically, but which relies on shapes, lines and colours for its appeal

avant-garde pioneers or innovators in any sphere of the arts

blackout turning off all visible lights to make targeting more difficult for enemy bombing missions

Blitz attempt by the German *Luftwaffe* (air force) to bomb British cities and civilian populations into surrender 1940–41

Bolshevist Russian name for a member of the Communist Party, used in Western countries to describe anyone suspected of supporting revolutionary communist ideals

cast image made by pouring a liquid that will harden, such as molten bronze, into a mould

classical art of Ancient Greece and Rome, or art done in that style

commission piece of work done at someone's request, usually for a fee

conscription compulsory military service

Cubism attempt to show all four dimensions – height, width, depth and time – in a two-dimensional art form. Cubism allowed the examination of an object from a variety of viewpoints, rather than the single viewpoint of traditional painting.

death duties taxes payable on a person's estate (property and belongings) after they have died

drape to cover with cloth or hangings

economic depression a slow-down in economic activity, usually signified by a rise in bankruptcies, high unemployment, low spending and political and social tension

empire large group of countries under the control of another country. Powerful countries with empires at this time included Britain, Germany and Austria-Hungary.

expansionism aim to increase the size and power of a country by invading others and colonizing them

Fascist ruling party in Italy 1922–43, which believed in extreme militarism and anti-communism

Festival of Britain event organized in 1951 to commemorate the centenary of the Great Exhibition of 1851, and demonstrate the British contribution to science, culture and the arts

figurative in the visual arts, a term describing art that is based on recognizable aspects of the world, in particular of the human form

found-and-altered objects removed from their natural setting and built into sculptures

grammar school school offering a high standard of education to pupils who pass exams taken at the age of eleven

graphic print, painting or illustration

lithograph type of hand-made print, made by putting oily dots on stone, covering them with water then ink and applying to paper

maquette small model of proposed larger sculpture

metaphor device in language or art where something is represented in terms of something else, such as the human body represented as landscape

Modernism name given to the art movement of the early 20th century, characterized by the use of unusual and unconventional subject matter

motif recurring theme or subject used by an artist

motive Moore's name for an upright figure resembling a totem pole

nationalist person who believes in the liberation of their country from invaders or foreign rulers, or someone who puts the interest of their nation above all else, and turns against outsiders, foreigners and minorities

Nazi belonging to the extreme right-wing anti-Semitic, anti-socialist and anti-communist political movement lead by Adolf Hitler, which took power in Germany in 1933

official war artist artist employed by the British government to record events in both World Wars

organic living, or relating to something living

pre-colonial term describing the societies and civilizations existing in the Americas and Africa before the arrival of European conquerors and settlers

primitive art early art of Latin America, Africa, Europe and the Pacific Islands

radical term describing intense and far-reaching political, social, cultural and artistic change

relief type of sculpture in which forms are raised from a flat surface, with only part of their depth showing

Renaissance term literally meaning 'rebirth', describing the explosion of art, science and philosophy in Italy in the 15th century. It signified the end of the period known as the Dark Ages.

retrospective exhibition showing the development of an artist's career and work to date

Russian Revolution revolution of 1917 in Russia in which the Communists, lead by Vladimir Lenin, took power and ended the rule of the Russian royal family

scholarship grant, or sum of money paid to a student of great promise or merit

slagheap mound of unusable rock and other material brought up during mining operations underground

slaughterhouse building where animals are killed for meat

Spanish Civil War conflict that engulfed Spain when the Spanish army, aided by Fascist Italy and Nazi Germany, rebelled against the elected Republican government in 1936

student teacher young person training to be a teacher. During the war, such students worked as teachers to cover the wartime shortages of adult teachers.

Sunday school schools run by churches, focusing on religious education

surrealist participant in the artistic movement called Surrealism, which promoted the use of humour, details from dreams and absurd mixtures of words and pictures

trench protective ditch dug for soldiers and laid out in lines facing the enemy, used particularly in World War I

trustee person who administers and oversees a trust fund or an institute to ensure it is run correctly

welfare state comprehensive health, social security and welfare system established in the UK in 1945 to rid the country of the worst effects of poverty and unemployment

working class people in a society whose only source of income is their labour, who have no money to invest in stocks and shares

Places of interest
and further reading

Websites

www.henry-moore-fdn.co.uk/hmf – The Henry Moore Foundation has information about Moore's life and work, the sculpture centre at Perry Green and the Henry Moore Institute in Leeds, UK. There are photographs, details of works on show and touring exhibitions. It also has links to other sites of interest.

www.leeds.gov.uk/tourinfo/attract/museums/moore.html – details of the sculpture collection held at the Henry Moore Sculpture Galleries of Leeds City Art Gallery. These include works by Moore, Jacob Epstein and Barbara Hepworth.

www.tate.org.uk – website of the Tate Galleries, which has a very comprehensive database of works by Moore, including photographs.

Further reading

Henry Moore in Public (The BBC in association with the Henry Moore Foundation, 1998)

A Monumental Vision: The Sculpture of Henry Moore, John Hedgecoe (Collins and Brown, London 1998)

Celebrating Moore: Works from the Collection of the Henry Moore Foundation, selected by David Mitchinson (Lund Humphries, London 1998)

Sources

Henry Moore – The Human Dimension (The Henry Moore Foundation in association with the British Council, 1991)

Henry Moore – My Ideas, Inspiration and Life as an Artist, Henry Moore and John Hedgcoe (Ebury Press, London 1986; Collins and Brown, London 1999)

Henry Moore – An Illustrated Biography, William Packer (Weidenfield and Nicolson, London 1985)

Henry Moore – Portrait of an Artist, John Read (Whizzard Press/André Deustch, London 1979)

Henry Moore, John Russell (The Penguin Press, London 1968)

Index